W9-CLB-674

DISCARD

DRINKING
A RISKY BUSINESS

DRINKING
A RISKY BUSINESS

LAURENCE PRINGLE

MORROW JUNIOR BOOKS • NEW YORK

Permission for the following photographs is gratefully acknowledged: AP/Wide World Photos, pp. 51, 52, 54, 59, 91; Children of Alcoholics Foundation, p. 41; Jeff Greenberg, Visuals Unlimited, pp. 2, 79; Manocherian Foundation, p. 76; Movie Star News, pp. 23, 33; National Council on Alcoholism and Drug Dependence, Inc., p. 96; New York Public Library Picture Collection, pp. 10, 12, 14, 22, 44, 50, 62; Felicia Schneberg, SADD, p. 89; United Distillers USA, Inc., p. 67; U.S. Department of Agriculture, p. 65; U.S. Department of Health and Human Services Administration, pp. 16, 30; U.S. Department of Transportation, p. 92. All other photographs by the author.

Original art on p. 21 by Ann Neumann.

Published by Morrow Junior Books
a division of William Morrow and Company, Inc.
1350 Avenue of the Americas, New York, NY 10019

Designed by Trish Parcell Watts.
Printed in the United States of America.

1 2 3 4 5 6 7 8 9 10

Library of Congress Cataloging-in-Publication Data
Pringle, Laurence P.
Drinking: a risky business/Laurence Pringle.
p. cm.
Includes bibliographical references and index.
Summary: Describes the history of alcohol, its effects on the body and personality, how to deal with peer pressure to drink, and how to get help for alcoholism.
ISBN: 0-688-15044-6
1. Alcoholism—Juvenile literature. [1. Alcohol 2. Alcoholism.] I. Title. HV5066.P75 1997 362.292—DC21 97-7807 CIP AC

CONTENTS

INTRODUCTION

"How about a drink?" "What can I get you?" "Want a beer?"

Each day these words are spoken millions of times across the country. Like oil and grease, which help moving metal parts in an engine work smoothly, alcoholic drinks are thought to help social events run well. Many feel these "social lubricants" are vital for helping people relax and have fun, whether at a dinner for two or a major party.

Alcoholic drinks are also served at countless other occasions, ranging from weddings to celebrations by professional sports teams upon winning a championship.

Sometimes it seems that everybody drinks. But that isn't true. While many millions do consume alcoholic beverages, other millions choose not to drink. About 29 percent of all people in the United States who are twenty-one or older do not. That's nearly a third of all adults. Somehow these people get along without the "social lubricants" that are so widespread.

Some nondrinkers avoid alcohol because they suffer from alcoholism. Some avoid it because of their religious beliefs. Many others choose not to drink for personal reasons. Perhaps they have a parent or other relative who is an alcoholic. Perhaps they had a friend or family member killed or maimed in an accident caused by drunken driving. In addition to those who avoid all alcohol, many millions know the dangers of drinking and are cautious in their consumption of alcohol.

Every year one hundred thousand people in the United States die as a direct result of alcohol consumption. What to do about alcohol is one of the toughest decisions faced by young people today. It is a particularly troubling question for children of alcoholics. Nearly seven million minors (people under eighteen years of age) in the United States have at least one alcoholic parent. Teenagers themselves also become alcoholics. And many teenagers find themselves with minds befuddled by alcohol at times—on a date or while driving—when clear thinking is vital.

The opportunities to drink will keep coming, so it makes sense to learn the facts about alcohol and drinking. This book discusses alcohol's origins and its short- and long-term effects on the brain and body, as well as its effects on the culture of the United States and other nations. It tells about the alcohol industry's promotion efforts, which offer no clues about the deaths and other harm caused by drinking. It also gives practical tips on drinking sensibly, or not drinking at all, for young people facing one of the most important health choices of their lives.

1 DISCOVERING ALCOHOL

"It prolongs life, clears away ill humors, revives the heart and maintains youth."

Arnauld de Villeneuve,
thirteenth-century physician, praising distilled liquor

Humans become drunk by consuming alcohol, but alcohol was produced naturally long before people inhabited the earth. Birds, bears, and other wild creatures—perhaps even dinosaurs—have become drunk from eating berries, other fruits, or grains containing alcohol.

Alcohol is produced when microscopic yeast spores digest sugars that are present in almost all fruits, grains, and vegetables. During this process, called fermentation, the yeast changes sugars to alcohol and carbon dioxide.

Humans somehow happened upon this natural process. In the case of wine making, the discovery was reportedly an accident. According to legend, King Dshemshid of Persia (now Iran), who ruled about five thousand years ago, was fond of grapes. He ordered his servants to store extra grapes in large jars. Months later, when he

Grapes and a goblet of wine shown on this ancient Greek pottery indicate that wine making has been practiced for thousands of years.

wanted the grapes, he was disappointed to learn that the grape skins had burst and the jars held a dark purple juice. He ordered the jars to be labeled POISON and stored in the cellar.

A woman who suffered from terrible headaches had decided to kill herself. She saw the jars labeled POISON and drank some of the liquid. She did not die. Instead she felt better. When she told the king about the effects of the juice, Dshemshid tried it himself. According to legend, from then on he had some of the annual grape harvest made into the alcoholic drink we call wine. He called it "royal medicine."

The first beer was also made in the Middle East, perhaps ten thousand years ago. Its production spread far and wide. Fermented barley is the grain usually used to make beer, although the ancient Chinese made a beer called kiu from a mixture of millet and rice. Beer making was especially popular in northern Europe, where the climate is too cold to grow the varieties of grapes from which wine was originally made. Also, beer is usually made from grains, so its ingredients are inexpensive. As such, beer has often been the drink of poor people.

In ancient Egypt, however, beer was consumed by both rich and poor. It was used as a religious offering and was buried in royal tombs. Egyptian writings more than four thousand years old include a father's warning to his student son about the danger of drinking too much beer.

On every continent inhabited by humans, people discovered ways of making beer or wine from grains, fruits, or other ingredients that were readily available. These alcoholic drinks probably didn't taste much like those of today. In addition, the methods of making them were primitive. Most beers, for example, were brewed in small batches and lasted only a few days before turning to vinegar.

In China, wine was made from rice. The emperor Yu is credited with learning how to make rice wine. Eventually he tried to outlaw its use. He feared that wine's effects on the population would lead to the fall of his kingdom. In Africa, wines and beers were made from corn, bananas, honey, millet, and many kinds of fruit. In southwestern North America, Native Americans made cactus wine.

In many cultures the use of wine and beer became part of everyday life. Wine was and still is used in religious ceremonies. People also drank alcoholic drinks because they were concerned—often with good reason—about the safety of drinking water from wells and rivers. Early beers did have some health benefits. Sailors who drank beer avoided scurvy, a disease caused by a lack of vitamin C during long voyages at sea. Ships began carrying beer for their crews. The *Mayflower,* which brought the Pilgrims to North America in 1620, also brought beer.

In the eighth century A.D. (about thirteen hundred years ago) a new kind of alcoholic drink was created by an Arabian alchemist named Jabir ibn Hayyan. He used a process now called distillation,

Beer was once considered a necessity for crews and passengers of sailing ships, including the Mayflower.

in which alcohol is separated from fermenting juices of grains, fruits, or vegetables. He boiled wine, capturing the vapors that were given off and cooling them so they returned to liquid form. Impurities were removed. The result was a liquid with a strong taste and high alcohol content. These distilled alcohols are called liquors.

In the thirteenth century A.D. a Spanish physician and alchemist, Arnauld de Villeneuve, distilled wine to make a liquor he called brandywine. Later it was simply called brandy. De Villeneuve thought he had created an extraordinary medicine and called brandy *agua vitae*—"water of life." He was not the first or the last physician to claim medical benefits for alcohol, especially for liquors. For several centuries, brandy and other liquors, now called cordials, were made almost exclusively for treating illness.

Gradually, knowledge of the process of distillation spread throughout Europe, and beyond. New kinds of liquors were produced. In Holland, the liquid from fermented barley was distilled to yield a drink called gin. Russians used fermented barley or potatoes to make vodka. Barley was also the source of whiskey in Ireland. Eventually, the Europeans who colonized eastern North America made whiskey from another grain, rye, and bourbon from a mixture of rye and corn. In Mexico, the liquor called tequila was made from the agave cactus.

The drink called rum can be made from fermented sugarcane or from molasses, the thick syrup created when white sugar is produced from sugarcane or sugar beets. Between 1650 and 1776 rum and molasses were key parts of the infamous Triangle Trade. The third part was African people who were captured to be slaves.

In colonial America,
drunks were sometimes
put in stationary or mobile stocks.

English ships carried them to the West Indies, where many of them
worked on the sugarcane plantations of Spanish or Portuguese
colonists. Ships then carried molasses from the West Indies to New

England. There rum was distilled from the molasses. The rum was then shipped to Africa, where it could be traded for more slaves, completing the triangle.

The Puritans who colonized New England believed that alcohol was God's gift to man. Many colonists used hard cider, beer, rum, or other alcoholic drinks as painkillers and as treatment for fevers, indigestion, and heart trouble. Alcohol was considered necessary and beneficial. However, records show there was another side to the story. Just a few years after the Plymouth Colony was established in what is now Massachusetts, a man named John Holmes was punished for drunkenness. He was forced "to sitt in the stocks, and was amerced forty shillings."

Troubles caused by drinking have existed for centuries. Although alcohol was once called "royal medicine," today we know that drinking alcohol can be a prescription for family troubles, poor health, and death.

Some people believe that beer is harmless, at least compared with liquor—a notion challenged in this poster from the U.S. Department of Health and Human Services.

2 ALCOHOL AND ITS EFFECTS

"Of the many types of alcohol, ethanol is the most intoxicating, the least toxic, and therefore the most commercially exploited. It is also the world's most widely used and abused psychoactive drug."

Scott E. Lucas,
Harvard Medical School

Many people drink alcohol as a beverage, as naturally as they eat food. And for many people, small amounts of alcohol may be harmless. It is wise to remember, however, that alcohol is a drug, a poison, a depressant. It is potentially dangerous, even deadly.

The alcohol commonly used in drinks is ethanol, or ethyl alcohol. There are other kinds of alcohol, including wood alcohol and rubbing alcohol, that are poisonous if swallowed, even in small amounts.

Drinking a lot of ethanol can be fatal as well. However, common alcoholic drinks contain only a small percent of ethyl alcohol. Beer contains the least amount, usually between 3 and 8 percent. So-called light beers contain about 2.5 to 2.7 percent alcohol. Wine contains between 8 and 20 percent alcohol. Wine coolers, now called low alcohol refreshers by the alcohol industry, contain about the same amount of alcohol as beer. (When first sold in the U.S., these drinks contained wine. Now most are malt beverages—brewed like beer—diluted with fruit juices and sugar.)

Liquors (sometimes called distilled spirits) contain high levels of alcohol—often between 40 and 50 percent and sometimes higher. Labels on liquor bottles reveal the alcohol content as a measure of "proof." One proof is a half percent (.5) alcohol. So a liquor labeled 80 proof is 40 percent alcohol (80 x .5 = 40).

Since the alcohol content of liquors is so high compared with that of beer and wine, they are usually served in a drink mixed with fruit juice, soda, tonic, or water (often in the form of ice cubes). A typical mixed drink made with such liquors as gin, rum, vodka, scotch, whiskey, or bourbon contains about one half to three-quarters of an ounce of alcohol. The same amount of alcohol is found in a 5-ounce glass of wine or in a 12-ounce bottle or can of beer or wine cooler.

Alcoholic drinks are high in calories. Mixed drinks with liquor often contain 300 calories. Five ounces of wine contain 150 calories; 12 ounces of beer, 170 calories. The calories in light beers range from 112 to 140 calories in 12 ounces. However, the calories in alcoholic drinks are what nutritionists often call "empty calories." By this they mean that alcohol produces energy but contains no vitamins, minerals, or other essential nutrients. Because heavy drinkers fill up on empty calories, they often don't eat regular meals or the amount and variety of foods needed for good health.

Poor nutrition is just one of many problems alcohol can cause. While the most dramatic effects take place in the brain, others occur throughout the body as alcohol is consumed, circulated, and digested. For example, alcohol irritates inner tissues it touches, beginning in the mouth and esophagus. It irritates the stomach lining, causing the release of gastric juices. If no food is present, these digestive chemicals can harm the stomach wall. People who frequently drink with an empty stomach often develop peptic ulcers, which are wounds in the stomach's lining caused by gastric juices.

Alcohol moves rapidly from the body's digestive system into the bloodstream. About 20 percent of alcohol consumed is absorbed into the bloodstream from the stomach. However, most of it—about 75 percent—is absorbed into the bloodstream through the walls of the upper area of the small intestine (where it may destroy digestive enzymes). Only about 5 percent leaves the body unchanged, in urine, sweat, or exhaled breath.

Once in the bloodstream, alcohol is carried rapidly to the heart. Since alcohol is a poison, or toxin, it stimulates the heart to beat more rapidly in an effort to get rid of the poison. This increases blood pressure. Drinking several ounces of alcohol a day can cause constant high blood pressure (hypertension). This stress on the heart can lead to heart failure.

Continuing through the bloodstream, alcohol reaches the liver. This is the only organ that breaks down alcohol. Enzymes act on alcohol molecules, changing them into water, carbon dioxide, and an acid called acetate that the body uses for energy. The process is called oxidation. The liver can oxidize about a third of an ounce of alcohol in an hour. If a person drinks more than this amount—remember, a l2-ounce can or bottle of beer contains half an ounce of alcohol— the remaining alcohol continues to circulate in the bloodstream.

The liver's job is to rid the body of poisons like alcohol. Ordinarily it can handle alcohol from moderate drinking without trouble. Difficulties arise, however, if a person drinks and also takes drugs, or drinks alcohol heavily. There are limits on the number and amounts of toxic substances a liver can handle without harm to it.

Years of heavy drinking can severely damage the liver. One liver disease that may develop is called alcoholic hepatitis. It strikes two or three days after a person consumes large amounts of alcohol. Its symptoms are nausea, vomiting, severe abdominal pain, and high fever. Alcoholic hepatitis can be fatal, though most patients recover. When a person continues to drink heavily, the hepatitis attacks occur more frequently.

A more serious liver disease may also result from heavy drinking—cirrhosis. Some drinkers have no warning that this liver disease is developing. In cirrhosis, cells of the liver are actually being killed by alcohol. When this happens, the organ loses its ability to break down alcohol and other toxic substances. Continued heavy drinking may cause the liver to fail entirely. If the liver becomes so damaged that it cannot rid the body of toxins—including ammonia, which is a normal by-product of food digestion—the drinker dies.

Of course, people do not begin to drink with the aim of harming their heart or liver, or with much knowledge about the risks involved. They drink to experience alcohol's effects on their brain.

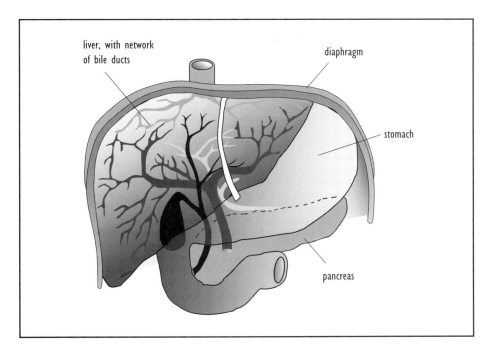

liver, with network of bile ducts

diaphragm

stomach

pancreas

The liver helps rid the body of harmful substances, including alcohol—a drug that can be fatal in large doses. A healthy liver can break down just a third of an ounce of alcohol in an hour.

Once in the bloodstream, alcohol reaches the brain quickly. The drug begins to affect nerve cells (neurons) in the brain. It slows the messages that travel along nerve fibers. Only a small amount of alcohol is needed to impair the normal performance of neurons, making a person slower to react and contributing to a feeling of relaxation.

Alcohol has one other effect on the brain. It causes blood vessels of the head to expand. This gives many people a kind of headache, called a hangover, after drinking. The headache eases when blood vessels around the brain return to normal size. Other hangover

Alcohol causes blood
vessels to expand, leading
to a hangover headache.

symptoms may include an upset stomach, shakiness, and sensitivity to light and sounds. Some people think they can cure a hangover by drinking coffee, taking a cold shower, eating sugar, or even having a little of the kind of alcoholic drink that led to their hangover (this is sometimes known as "the hair of the dog that bit you"). But the only cure for a hangover is the time needed for enlarged blood vessels to shrink.

Some people believe that alcohol is a stimulant, since after a drink or two they "loosen up" and feel more relaxed and sociable. But alcohol is a drug that actually depresses the workings of the brain, including the areas of the brain that control judgment and movements. It alters perceptions and emotions, vision, hearing, and coordination. Depending on the amount of alcohol consumed (and other factors described below) a person's brain may become so impaired that we say the person is drunk. (Other terms for this condition are "intoxicated" and "inebriated." Still others are listed in the box on the next page.)

Everyone recognizes the stereotypical image of a drunk person, with slurred speech, faulty vision, poor coordination, and unsteady feet. Frequently, the role of a drunk is played for laughs in movies

Is drunken behavior funny? It is often presented that way in movies and on television.

MANY WAYS OF BEING DRUNK

Besides being inebriated or intoxicated,
a drunken person is sometimes said to be:

besotted	polluted
blasted	potted
blotto	ripped
bombed	sloshed
boozy	smashed
crapulent	sotted
crocked	soused
feeling no pain	stewed
hammered	stinko
high as a kite	tanked
lit	three sheets to the wind
lit to the gills	tight
loaded	tipsy
looped	under the influence
lubricated	under the table
pickled	wasted
plastered	zonked

As a result of being in this condition, many thousands of people can be said to be "dead," "dead as a doornail," "deceased," and so on.

and on television, but countless viewers who have suffered losses as a result of drunkenness fail to see the humor.

The amount of alcohol that causes an individual to become drunk varies with each person. The key factor is the concentration of alcohol in the blood, and this is affected by several factors. One is the size of the drinker. A small person has less blood in his or her circulatory system than a big person. Therefore, a given amount of alcohol in his or her blood is more concentrated than in the blood of a larger person. So small adults can become intoxicated even if they drink less than large adults.

Women usually weigh less than men, and since pound for pound they have more fat and less water, alcohol is more concentrated in their blood. Also, the livers of women process alcohol less efficiently than those of men. These factors make women more susceptible than men to harm from alcohol. And since teenagers usually weigh less than adults, alcohol is likely to affect them more than adults.

Drinking with an empty stomach also increases the possibility of becoming drunk. When the stomach and small intestine have little or no food to digest, whatever amount of alcohol an individual consumes enters the bloodstream rapidly.

Drinking a lot in a short time also leads to intoxication. The liver cannot rid the body of all the alcohol quickly, so a large amount continues to circulate in the blood and reach the brain. In contrast, the same amount of alcohol consumed over several hours may have little effect.

Although there is no question about intoxication when a person is falling-down drunk, there are degrees of drunkenness or impairment. A person can be mildly or strongly intoxicated, or somewhere in between. What determines the degree of impairment is the concentration of alcohol in the blood. This is the factor used by the legal system in enforcing laws against drunken driving. And because the amount of alcohol in a person's breath is also a good indicator of the degree of drunkenness, devices that measure alcohol in exhaled air are commonly used in law enforcement.

Consuming a small amount of alcohol may cause some subtle effects on a person's behavior and perceptions. As the functioning of the drinker's brain slows down, alcohol's effects as a social lubricant may begin to work. The person usually feels more relaxed and less anxious and as a result may become less shy, more talkative. Most people find this a pleasurable experience, and this is why many people drink alcohol. Interestingly, studies described on page 97 have shown that these pleasant feelings can occur when people only *believe* they have consumed alcohol.

A blood alcohol concentration (BAC) of only .05 percent (one twentieth of 1 percent) begins to impair thoughts and judgments and may affect vision. A driver with this BAC makes increased steering errors.

At a BAC of .08 percent, a drinker's motor skills—control of muscle movements—become seriously impaired. The time needed to react increases. At .10 percent, the reaction time increases even more, and a person's movements become noticeably clumsy. In most states it is illegal to drive with a blood alcohol concentration of .10 percent.

At an alcohol concentration of .20 percent, the part of the brain that controls movements is almost shut down. The drinker staggers and has trouble standing and walking. Speech may be slurred and confused. The part of the brain that controls emotions is also depressed by alcohol. The drinker's normal inhibitions may disappear, and underlying emotions may be expressed. Some people feel extremely happy, others sad. Some become "mean drunks"—rowdy, nasty, abusive, violent.

When the BAC reaches .30 percent, a drinker cannot track a moving object with his or her eyes. The person becomes confused and may pass out, or may stay conscious but later have no memory of what occurred. This alcohol-induced "blackout," as it is called, is particularly scary, as the drinker can learn only from others about his or her drunken words and actions.

At a blood alcohol concentration of .40 percent, the drinker becomes unconscious and may go into a coma. At .50 percent, the workings of the brain are so depressed that breathing stops, and the person usually dies of acute alcohol poisoning.

Each year several thousand people die of acute alcohol poisoning in the United States alone. At least eight hundred of the victims are high school and college students. Again, because they generally weigh less than adults, young people are more vulnerable to alcohol.

In one case a sixteen-year-old boy died after quickly drinking a pint of vodka. In another, a seventeen-year-old girl went to a party that was promoted as offering "all you can drink for $5" after high school graduation. She consumed seventeen drinks before she passed out. Her older sister took her home and put her to bed. Her mother found her dead in the morning.

RECOGNIZING ALCOHOL POISONING

SYMPTOMS:

- The person is semiconscious or unconscious and cannot be awakened.
- The person's skin is cold and either pale or bluish.
- The person's breathing is slow, less than eight times a minute, or irregular, with ten seconds or more between breaths.
- The person vomits while sleeping or passed out and does not wake up.

ACTIONS:

A person with any of the above symptoms may be suffering from acute alcohol poisoning. The actions you take may save a life.

- Turn the person on his or her side to prevent choking on vomit.
- Do not leave the person alone.
- Get help. Call an adult, an ambulance, or 911.

Source: Remove Intoxicated Drivers (RID-USA)

Some young people do not die directly from alcohol poisoning; they die from suffocating. One of the human body's defenses against a heavy dose of alcohol is to rid the stomach of the poison by vomiting. Each year scores of teenagers die after going to bed to "sleep off" the effects of their heavy drinking. They vomit while asleep, their breathing passages become clogged, and they die from lack of oxygen.

Everybody—even people who do not drink and those who drink moderate amounts of alcohol—needs to know about the risks of heavy drinking. Knowing about them may help save someone's life. (See the box on the previous page about alcohol poisoning.)

Drinking alcohol may give some people a pleasant sensation. But remember: Alcohol is a poison. Drinking too much, too fast, can kill you.

The typical alcoholic American

Doctor, age 54

Farmer, age 35

Unemployed, age 40

College student, age 19

Counselor, age 38

Retired editor, age 86

Dancer, age 22

Police officer, age 46

Military officer, age 31

Student, age 14

Executive, age 50

Taxi driver, age 61

Homemaker, age 43

Bricklayer, age 29

Computer programmer, age 25

Lawyer, age 52

There's no such thing as typical. We have all kinds.
10 million Americans are alcoholic.
It's our number one drug problem.

For information or help, contact:
National Clearinghouse for Alcohol and Drug Information, P.O. Box 2345, Rockville, MD 20852
1–800–729–6686

Young or old, rich or poor, anyone can be an alcoholic, as shown in this poster from the U.S. Department of Health and Human Services.

3 THE TERRIBLE TOLL OF ALCOHOLISM

"Don't trust. Don't talk. Don't feel. This is the credo of children of alcoholics."

Migs Woodside, President,
Children of Alcoholics Foundation

One out of ten adults in the United States suffers from alcoholism. Out of an estimated 28.6 million people who have at least one parent who is an alcoholic, nearly 7 million are children or teenagers. The children of alcoholics are three and a half times more likely than others to become alcoholics themselves.

When people are asked to describe an alcoholic, they often picture a "bum"—a man in shabby clothes, unshaven and with bloodshot eyes, who begs for money on a sidewalk. This may be the stereotypical image, but in reality, *anyone* can become an alcoholic. An alcoholic can be rich or poor, male or female, young or old. An alcoholic can be a well-to-do woman in her beautiful home. An alcoholic can be a twelve-year-old kid.

There is no single cause of alcoholism. Since a given amount of alcohol affects different people in different ways, there are no hard-

and-fast statistics that indicate how much or how often alcohol must be consumed in order to cause alcoholism. In fact, there is even some debate about a correct definition of this condition. Alcoholism is generally defined as a dependence on alcohol that interferes with normal life: work (including schoolwork), social life, family and other personal relationships. Anyone having alcohol-related problems in these basic parts of life may be an alcoholic.

Alcoholism usually involves habitual excessive drinking. But because not all alcoholics drink heavily, Alcoholics Anonymous, an international self-help group, uses a broader definition of the term "alcoholic." AA says an alcoholic is "anyone who feels that he or she has a problem with alcohol and wants to stop drinking."

Identifying the origins of alcoholism is as complex a matter as defining it. For example, statistics indicate that alcoholism runs in families. In other words, having an alcoholic parent increases the risk that a young person will also have drinking problems. Someone with both an alcoholic mother and an alcoholic father is even more likely to become an alcoholic.

While these facts do not prove there is an "alcoholism gene" that is passed from one generation to the next, some research does suggest that alcohol-related problems may be inherited. In 1996, genetic researchers at the Veteran's Affairs Medical Center in Portland, Oregon, found that the absence of a certain gene was enough to turn healthy laboratory mice into heavy drinkers.

Other research results announced in 1996 also suggest that people can inherit a tendency to become alcoholics. In a study conducted at the University of California at San Diego, it was learned

Sometimes a movie gives a realistic view of an alcoholic's self-destructive behavior, as shown in the film classic Days of Wine and Roses.

that men who had a low response to alcohol—which is an inherited trait—were in greater danger of having drinking problems than other men. Because these men needed to drink more than others to feel an effect from alcohol, they were more likely than average to become alcoholics later in life, even if they drank small amounts of alcohol earlier. In this study the riskiest situation was to have an alcoholic father and also a low response to alcohol. These men had a 60 percent chance of becoming alcoholics.

In addition to genetic risk factors for alcoholism, other factors are likely to be involved. For example, parents are powerful role models for their children. Even though children often suffer greatly from living with an alcoholic parent, they may adopt certain attitudes and behavior that eventually lead them to be alcoholics themselves. If they see a parent reach for a bottle as a solution to the problems of life, for instance, they may do the same unless they learn other ways of coping instead.

Some psychologists contend that there is an "alcoholic personality"—a set of behavioral traits that makes a person highly vulnerable to drinking. Alcoholics are often described as being immature and easily frustrated. They are also said to have poor defenses against stress and anxiety. However, not all people with such characteristics have drinking problems—and drinking problems sometimes develop in people who seem mature and generally deal well with stress. Therefore, there is no strong evidence that alcoholism arises from any specific personality type.

Until the twentieth century, people with drinking problems were considered moral failures. It was believed that they drank because of character flaws; they were therefore scolded and punished. By the mid-twentieth century a new perspective had taken hold: Alcoholism was a disease, and those suffering from it should get treatment. However, alcoholism is unlike other diseases, and today many scientists prefer to call it an addiction—a powerful dependence on a substance. In their book *Alcohol: Use and Abuse in America,* Harvard University professors Jack Mendelson and Nancy Mello wrote, "Like it or not, alcohol is, and always has been, a drug and an intoxicant.... Moreover, it is addicting, as evidenced by the fact that withdrawal signs and symptoms occur after repeated severe or prolonged intoxication."

According to the American Psychiatric Association, there are several factors to consider in determining whether a substance is addictive. One is a physical or psychological dependence on the substance. Another is the unpleasant physical symptoms that arise when a person goes without the substance. And a third is a tolerance for the substance that the user develops. Alcoholics experience all of these symptoms. In the case of tolerance, people must drink more and more to reach the changes in mood and behavior they once reached with small amounts of alcohol. Eventually, an alcoholic often shows little outward sign of a high alcohol blood level.

Whatever its origins, alcoholism's effects are devastating. From a physical standpoint alone, alcoholics pay a heavy price. Alcoholism is the third-greatest killer in the United States, after heart disease and cancer. Heavy drinking adds to the cancer death rate, particularly for cancers of the digestive tract. An alcoholic is also two to five times more likely than a moderate drinker to develop cancer of the pharynx, larynx, and esophagus; and his or her risk of liver cancer is even greater. While alcohol itself does not seem to cause cancer, it weakens the body's defenses against this disease. In addition, many alcoholics are also smokers, and the combination of poisons taken into their bodies contributes to many deaths by cancer and heart failure.

In addition to high blood pressure and to cirrhosis of the liver, alcoholics frequently suffer from damage to the brain and nervous system. This becomes plain when they choose to, or are forced to, go without alcohol. They feel anxious. Their arms and hands may shake. They may not be able to sleep or, if they do, they may have nightmares and hallucinations. These symptoms of withdrawal from alcohol usually begin to appear a few hours after going without a drink.

Some alcoholics suffer from a more severe reaction to being without alcohol called delirium tremens, or "the DTs." The alcoholic trembles and sweats, feels confused and disoriented, and has vivid hallucinations. The DTs usually occur within three to five days of being without the drug alcohol and are sometimes fatal.

Drinkers sometimes joke about alcohol killing their brain cells. This is a fact, and something that a light drinker might laugh off because the brain is made up of about ten billion neurons and the loss of a small percentage of the total has no noticeable effect. Long-term heavy drinking, however, may destroy between 20 and 30 percent of a person's brain cells. Autopsies of alcoholics reveal shrunken brains that are below normal weight.

In years past, alcohol alone used to be blamed for the memory loss and other mental difficulties from which alcoholics suffer. However, some of the most common impairment is now known to be caused by a lack of thiamine (vitamin B_1). The vitamin deficiency occurs because heavy drinkers often have poor diets, and also because alcohol interferes with the normal digestion of foods that provide thiamine.

In addition to the pain and suffering alcoholics cause themselves, they are also a huge burden on society. In fact, alcoholism has been called a social plague. Alcoholics fail to show up for work, add to health care costs, and injure or kill others while attempting to drive. They also inflict great damage on their families—according to crime statistics, 52 percent of all spouse abusers have a history of alcoholism.

Physical violence, however, is far from the only harm alcoholics do in families. Some of the physical damage done to children of alcoholics begins early—even before they are born. Any woman who drinks heavily while pregnant endangers the health of her developing baby.

This damage occurs because alcohol in the mother's blood enters the womb (placenta) that surrounds the embryo or fetus. (For the first two months a developing baby is called an embryo; after that it is called a fetus.) An embryo or fetus is defenseless against alcohol, because the organ that rids its body of alcohol—its liver—is not completely developed until about the time of birth. The result is damage to the health of the fetus, and sometimes death. Alcoholic women also harm their developing young because they may have poor nutrition. Furthermore, many of them smoke cigarettes, a proven source of poisons that reach the womb and that also reduce the amount of vital oxygen available to the embryo or fetus.

It is not possible to tell which of these threats causes specific problems for an infant born to an alcoholic mother. Nevertheless, people have long suspected that alcohol could harm developing babies—warnings against drinking by pregnant women can be found in the Bible. In the mid-twentieth century, medical researchers began to study and report their observations of children born to alcoholic mothers. Their reports described abnormal

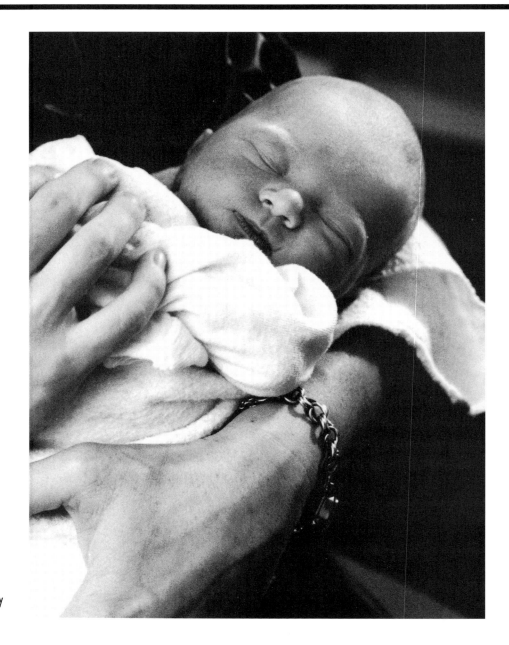

A pregnant woman who drinks alcohol puts the health of her developing baby at risk.

behavior and appearance, low intelligence scores, hyperactivity, and social problems.

In the 1980s these characteristics were assigned a name: fetal alcohol syndrome (FAS). Newborns with FAS have below-normal weight, so some die as infants. Those who survive have many infections, because their immune systems (which normally help fend off diseases) have been weakened by exposure to alcohol. In the United States, FAS is the third most common cause of mental retardation.

One out of three children born to alcoholic mothers suffers from fetal alcohol syndrome. The incidence in the general population is much smaller: Depending on the population studied, the rate of FAS ranges from 1 in 300 to 1 in 2,000 live births. Fortunately, if alcoholic mothers reduce their level of drinking while pregnant, the harm to their babies is decreased.

People wonder if pregnant women should drink at all. Scientists who study FAS say there is no known safe amount of alcohol. The quantity of alcohol necessary to harm an embryo or fetus is unknown. While occasional alcohol use may be safe, pregnant women are advised to be cautious. In fact, since 1989 warning signs have been posted where alcohol is served in the United States, and warning labels are required on containers of alcoholic beverages. The signs and labels say:

> GOVERNMENT WARNING: (1) According to the Surgeon General, women should not drink alcoholic beverages during pregnancy because of the risk of birth defects. (2) Consumption of alcoholic beverages impairs your ability to drive a car or operate machinery, and may cause health problems.

In addition to the physical damage associated with FAS, a child can be scarred for life by simply being part of a family with an alcoholic parent. Part of the scarring may be the results of physical beatings and sexual abuse. But even without such assaults, emotional scarring is possible. Having an alcoholic parent may leave a child feeling anxious, frustrated, guilty, and sad.

One characteristic of alcoholic families is that children learn to hide the problem. Jay David, editor of *The Family Secret: Adult Children of Alcoholics Tell Their Stories,* wrote, "They become experts at hiding the secret of parental drinking and making excuses for outrageous behavior.... The habit of secrecy and avoiding problems often carries over into adulthood, even when the alcoholism doesn't."

One contributor to *The Family Secret,* author Joyce Maynard, wrote of growing up in an alcoholic household: "As difficult as it was dealing with my father's drinking, the greater pain for me was the secret keeping. Adult children of alcoholics refer to the phenomenon as 'the elephant in the living room': You have a huge inescapable fact about your life that affects everything in your home, but nobody mentions it, although everybody's behavior is altered to accommodate or deal with it."

Since the reality of alcoholism is denied in most alcoholic families, children in such families have trouble knowing what is real and what is not. Usually they feel they cannot trust their alcoholic parent, so they may learn not to trust anyone, and not to trust their own feelings. Additionally, their family life may turn chaotic at any time, with random violence by a drunken parent,

LEFT: To an alcoholic, alcohol comes first, family second, as shown in this drawing by a teenager that was made into a poster by the Children of Alcoholics Foundation.

BELOW: This drawing by a thirteen-year-old illustrates some of the emotional damage suffered by children of alcoholics.

so their home is a place of stress and tension.

Emotional stress can affect the health of these children, giving them headaches and stomachaches. They suffer from more sickness and injuries than other children. They spend more time in hospitals.

Children from alcoholic homes carry a heavy burden out into the world. They often have difficulty concentrating in school and in forming friendships. According to the Children of Alcoholics Foundation, teenage children of alcoholics are three times more likely than others to drop out of school or to be expelled. On the other hand, some children of alcoholics become perfectionists and "mini-adults." They are robbed of their childhood because they take over responsibilities an alcoholic parent (or parents) cannot handle. They may excel at school, partly just to maintain the illusion that everything is fine at home. Other children in an alcoholic family may adopt other roles. (For more details about this, see "Sources of Helpful Information," pages 103–4.)

In a sense, an alcoholic parent is an absent parent. At times he or she may be physically absent because of drinking, but even when the individual is home, he or she is not emotionally available to the family. The alcoholic's main relationship is his or her addiction to the drug alcohol. Everything and everyone else is secondary.

Ironically, children of alcoholics often lose twice—first by having an alcoholic parent, then by the early death of that parent. Alcoholism cuts lives short. For some children this is actually a blessing and a great relief, but of course most alcoholic parents have good qualities that their children sorely miss.

Although children of alcoholics are at risk of becoming alcoholics themselves, the majority do not. Their home experience may actually give them strength and some coping skills that help them lead satisfying lives as adults. However, there is no denying the terrible toll of alcoholism—on families, society, and the addicted drinkers themselves.

Alcohol abuse was common in the young United States, and Benjamin Rush is credited with starting a movement that eventually led to the complete prohibition of liquor.

4 TRYING TO OUTLAW ALCOHOL

"Mother's in the kitchen, washing out the jugs;

Sister's in the pantry, bottling the suds;

Father's in the cellar, mixing up the hops;

Johnny's on the front porch, watching for the cops."

Anonymous poem written in the 1920s,
during Prohibition

When the thirteen American colonies declared their freedom from England on July 4, 1776, Benjamin Rush signed his name on the Declaration of Independence. He is best remembered, however, for his campaign against drinking. A well-known and respected doctor, Rush was alarmed by the drunkenness that was so common in the new nation.

Rush wrote a booklet, *An Inquiry into the Effects of Ardent Spirits upon the Human Mind and Body,* that warned of the dangers of drinking liquor. Although he encouraged consumption of beer and wine, claiming that these drinks led to good health and wealth, he wrote that distilled spirits led to disease—liver problems, diabetes, gout, madness—and frequent belching. The doctor also described the effects on the behavior of a rum or whiskey drinker: "In folly it causes him to resemble a calf; in stupidity, an ass; in roaring, a mad bull; in quarreling and fighting, a dog; in cruelty, a tiger; in fetor, a skunk; in filthiness, a hog; and in obscenity, a he-goat."

Benjamin Rush was not the only person warning of the evils of drinking. As a result of his efforts and those of others, some citizens formed groups called temperance societies in the early 1800s. At that time temperance meant using alcohol moderately and wisely. However, some members went so far as to pledge to give up *all* alcohol for a year, unless it was needed for health reasons.

This qualification reflected the notions about alcohol in those times. Many people believed that alcoholic drinks, especially liquor, warded off fevers and illness. Laborers, soldiers, sailors, and many other workers were given daily rations of rum or whiskey. Doctors routinely prescribed alcoholic drinks as a treatment for disease.

However, the people who abstained from alcohol for a year or more learned a remarkable truth—that they felt better and worked better. As described in Jack Mendelson and Nancy Mello's book *Alcohol: Use and Abuse in America,* "When the trial period had ended, the abstainers met again to voice their surprise that houses could be built, barns could be raised, grain could be harvested, christenings could be enjoyed, and the dead could be mourned without the constant accompaniment of distilled spirits."

Members of early temperance groups began giving speeches and distributing pamphlets to educate others about the benefits of giving up alcohol. They urged farmers and other employers to end the practice of giving free liquor to their workers. They argued, correctly, that excessive drinking reduced the effectiveness of employees and caused accidents and absenteeism.

Ministers and other members of the clergy joined the anti-drinking crusade. One of the most outspoken and effective was the Reverend Lyman Beecher of Connecticut, a dynamic speaker and writer. He condemned all alcoholic drinks and denounced even moderate drinking. He believed that alcohol was a poison; therefore there could be no "prudent use." Reverend Beecher's words inspired many thousands of people to join the temperance movement. His arguments also changed the accepted meaning of the word "temperance." In 1836 the American Temperance Society agreed with the reverend and officially changed its definition of temperance to mean abstinence—giving up drinking all alcoholic beverages.

The efforts of temperance groups were opposed by liquor makers, saloon keepers, and others who profited from alcohol sales. Even more powerful opposition came from society at large. After the American Revolution, rum and especially whiskey were cheap, and heavy drinking had become part of the culture. Historians estimate that until about 1830, American adults consumed an average of 7 gallons of pure alcohol annually, or 2.5 ounces of alcohol *per day.* (Remember, alcoholic drinks are not pure alcohol; even a powerful 100-proof liquor is only half alcohol.) To put these numbers in perspective, consider that adults in the United States now drink an average of 2.7 gallons of pure alcohol each year. People in 1830 consumed two and a half times that amount. No wonder the Reverend Ebenezer Porter of Connecticut had called the young

United States "a nation of drunkards" in 1805.

The temperance movement gained momentum because many Americans had firsthand experience with alcohol abuse in their families or neighborhoods and agreed that change was needed. By 1835, more than thirty-five thousand Protestant ministers had signed a pledge to give up liquor. In 1851 the state of Maine enacted a law that prohibited the distilling and sale of liquor within its borders. By 1855, thirteen of forty states and territories then making up the United States had established similar laws. About a third of the U.S. population lived under prohibition laws like that of Maine.

This was the peak of the nineteenth-century antidrinking crusade. During the Civil War, people fighting for social change were more concerned with ending slavery than endorsing temperance. The federal government raised money from a tax on liquor and did nothing to discourage its use. Courts found some prohibition laws unconstitutional; one by one, states repealed them. And heavy drinking of whiskey in saloons became part of the lives of laborers and other workers, both on the western frontier and in the growing urban centers.

Although public opinion about alcohol may have become more accepting, the next great antidrinking crusade was beginning to grow. This time the driving force was women. Alcohol was seen as a threat to home and family, and women were viewed as their protectors. In 1873 a movement that came to be known as the Women's Crusade began in Ohio and New York. Believing that alcohol abuse and the sale of alcohol were moral issues, the women tried to sway onlookers against saloons. By late 1874 a national convention of the

Women's Crusade included groups from sixteen states. The fast-growing organization was renamed the Women's Christian Temperance Union (WCTU).

The WCTU began as a temperance praying society in which groups of women prayed and sang hymns. By the late 1870s it had become an active political lobbying group—the first mass movement of women in United States politics. While it supported the right of women to vote, it is best known for its antidrinking efforts. As Yale University historian Dr. David Musto wrote in 1996, women "could reasonably argue that they had a duty to oppose alcohol and saloons—which were efficiently separating men from their paychecks and turning them into menaces to their families."

In the 1880s the WCTU was powerful enough to cause some states to pass prohibition laws, and by 1900, to put in place mandatory lessons in the public schools of most states about the dangers of alcohol. Children were taught that "alcohol clogs the brain and turns the liver quickly from yellow to green to black."

Although the WCTU still exists today, early in the twentieth century its leading role against alcohol was taken over by the Anti-Saloon League—perhaps the most powerful citizens' pressure group in American history. Its goal was to outlaw alcoholic beverages, but it wisely aimed first at saloons. It built support at the local and state levels, promoting laws that prohibited Sunday alcohol sales and serving alcohol to minors. The Anti-Saloon League gave strong support to political candidates who would work for prohibition laws, including the rights of towns, cities, and counties to adopt prohibition.

The temperance movement gained strength because many people, especially women, could see the terrible toll that alcohol took on families.

By 1916 twenty-three states had prohibited making or selling liquor. (Personal use of beer and wine was usually allowed.) As for ending the consumption of liquor, however, the fact that some states were "dry" (prohibiting liquor) and others "wet" (allowing liquor) led to a lively interstate liquor business. The solution to this problem, said the leaders of the Anti-Saloon League, was a national prohibition law. So in 1913 the league proposed an amendment to the U.S. Constitution that would prohibit "the sale, manufacture for sale, transportation for sale, importation for sale, and exportation for sale, of intoxicating liquors for beverage purposes in the United States."

The amendment was opposed by liquor dealers and others who had a financial stake in the liquor industry. In 1914 the amendment fell short of the two-thirds majority vote needed in Congress. However, the Anti-Saloon League worked tirelessly to help elect legislators who favored prohibition. In late 1917 a modified version of the prohibition amendment passed handily in both the U.S. Senate and

Temperance groups came to promote the idea that moderate drinking led inevitably to drunkenness and alcoholism.

"HUH, I CAN DRINK or LET IT ALONE!"
"THAT'S WHAT I THOUGHT, TOO."
MODERATE DRINKING IS THE TAPROOT OF DRUNKENESS
OHIO ANTI-SALOON LEAGUE

Women played a key role in the political battles that led to tougher laws on sales of alcohol and eventually to Prohibition.

the House of Representatives. Then came the final challenge: ratification of the Constitutional amendment by at least thirty-five states within seven years. The Anti-Saloon League's expertise at working with state legislators helped achieve this goal in record time. The Eighteenth Amendment—Prohibition—became law on January 16, 1919.

Historians and social scientists continue to analyze why Prohibition became law in the United States. They generally conclude that, at a time of rapid changes due to industrialization and urban growth, many citizens wanted to protect home and family, and getting rid of saloons was seen as a way to do that. Many were also convinced that outlawing liquor would help rid America of disease and poverty. The United States was not alone in trying to make social reforms by forbidding liquor. Many European nations also passed prohibition laws early in the twentieth century.

There is no doubt that Prohibition had positive effects in the United States. An estimated one hundred seventy thousand saloons went out of business. The annual death rate from cirrhosis of the liver dropped dramatically. So did arrests for drunkenness and hospital admissions for alcohol-related illness. But overall, the "Great Experiment," as it was called, was a failure. Within a few years many people began breaking the law. Liquor was smuggled (by "bootleggers") into the United States from abroad or was made from illegal liquor distilleries operating within the country (by "moonshiners"). Secret hideaway bars called speakeasies sprang up. Organized crime flourished.

Many people had supported Prohibition because they thought that the sale of beer and wine would be permitted. However, court decisions set the alcohol content of "intoxicating liquors" at 5 percent. As a result, brewers began producing beer with a low alcohol content. "Near beer," as it was sometimes called, didn't satisfy most beer drinkers. The comedian Will Rogers said, "Whoever called it near beer was a mighty poor judge of distance."

Illegal liquor was very expensive, too costly for most laborers, so people began brewing beer, making wine, and even distilling liquors

Law enforcement agents destroyed many distilleries during Prohibition, but the illegal liquor trade still flourished.

at home. Within a few years, many middle- and upper-income people began to view drinking liquor as fashionable and sophisticated—and all the more alluring because it was forbidden.

Although the prison population in the United States doubled in the early 1920s, law enforcement agencies could not stop the flood of smuggled liquor or destroy every illegal distillery. Payoffs and bribes of officials were common. Leaders of criminal gangs, made rich from bootlegging, became romantic heroes to some. Clearly, Prohibition was not fixing the social ills of America.

Some of the same influential people who had advocated Prohibition began to call for its repeal. In 1932 the Democratic presidential candidate, Franklin D. Roosevelt, promised repeal of Prohibition if he was elected. Shortly after becoming president, Roosevelt legalized beer sales. First Congress and soon the states approved the Twenty-first Amendment to the Constitution. Officially adopted in December 1933, it repealed Prohibition and left all regulation of alcohol sales to the states.

One result of the Twenty-first Amendment was a patchwork of state and local liquor laws. Long after national Prohibition ended, more than a dozen states stayed dry. The last state to end prohibition, Mississippi, did so in 1966. In most states local governments could choose to be dry or wet. These differences continue today across the United States. Some states have a system of issuing licenses for manufacturers and sellers of alcoholic drinks; in other states, the government itself controls the sale of alcohol.

Even though much more is known today about the harm done by alcohol, national Prohibition is not likely to be tried again. For one thing, the 1919–33 experience showed that outright prohibition of alcohol use is not an effective long-term way to prevent alcohol abuse. For another, we now have a better understanding of alcohol's effects. We know that light or even moderate drinking is probably harmless for adults. In contrast, many members of temperance groups and advocates of prohibition believed the preaching of the Reverend Lyman Beecher—that a few drinks led inevitably down a slippery slope to drunkenness and alcoholism.

In the decades following repeal of Prohibition, alcohol consumption stayed near an annual average of 2.7 gallons of pure alcohol per adult. While this may not seem like a great quantity, remember that twenty-nine out of a hundred adults do not drink, so some adults consume considerably more than others. In fact, it is estimated that half of all the alcohol consumed in the United States is drunk by just 6 to 7 percent of the population. Furthermore, since it is illegal for anyone under twenty-one to buy alcoholic drinks, the usual national drinking statistics do not reflect drinking by minors.

Drinking patterns have changed in the twentieth century. Wine has grown in popularity and is often consumed at meals, as it has been traditionally consumed in France and Italy for many centuries. Beer has also become more popular. In 1990 beer accounted for 54.7 percent of all alcohol consumed in the United States, wine for 13.5 percent, and liquor for 31.8 percent. Since 1980 liquor sales have dropped nearly 30 percent. Wine consumption has fallen 6 percent. In the same period, consumption of beer has increased about 4 percent, thanks in part to small microbrewing companies that offer scores of new brands. Sales of low-alcohol near beer have also grown. Overall, however, alcohol consumption has declined. A 1995 Gallup poll asked adults about their drinking over the past five years. Seven percent said they had drunk more, but 41 percent said they had consumed less.

Social scientists expect alcohol consumption to continue dropping in the United States. One reason is the aging of the population. People over sixty tend to cut back on drinking or abstain; this segment of the population is growing. Another reason is that people are tending to drink wine or beer rather than liquor, with its much higher alcohol content. Finally, the strong interest in health, fitness, and good nutrition is expected to continue.

The popularity of beers from many so-called microbreweries has caused a rise in beer consumption, though overall alcohol consumption in the United States has declined in recent years.

Even though alcohol consumption has declined and is likely to drop further, public concern about alcohol is growing. The cost of alcoholism and alcohol abuse—in money, health, and lives—is still enormous.

The economic cost of alcohol abuse includes medical care, treatment, and rehabilitation; reduced or lost worker productivity; and expenses of law enforcement. According to a 1990 study, the economic cost was $98.6 billion, an increase of 40 percent since 1985. Alcohol abuse also causes great pain and suffering—harm that cannot be calculated in dollars and cents.

Especially worrisome is alcohol consumption by young people.

A DEADLY DRINK

Despite a decline in drinking in the United States, in the mid-1990s use of alcohol was estimated to be involved in:

- 70 percent of all murders
- 70 percent of boating accidents
- 60 percent of sex crimes against children
- 60 percent of child abuse cases
- 53 percent of fire deaths
- 50 percent of emergency room cases on weekend nights

- 50 percent of rapes
- 45 percent of drownings
- 44.6 percent of traffic fatalities
- 41 percent of assaults
- 37 percent of suicides
- 30 percent of fatal falls

Source: IDEA (Illinois Drug Education Alliance)

Alcohol is the number one drug abuse problem for American youth. About fifty years ago, in 1948, only 35 percent of high school students drank. Now many more minors take up drinking; they also begin drinking earlier. One survey of fourth graders found that a third of them reported pressure from their peers to try an alcoholic drink. Twenty-five percent of eighth graders reported that they had used alcohol in the past month. According to a 1994 study, about 1 percent of eighth graders, 2 percent of tenth graders, and 3 percent of twelfth graders claimed that they drank *every day.* One percent of high school seniors said they got drunk every day.

The tragic loss of young lives, especially from drunk driving, has led to tougher laws and school programs aimed to teach teenagers about the risks of drinking. A number of concerned people believe that further steps are needed to turn minors away from alcohol abuse. While some social scientists wonder whether the United States is heading into a third wave of temperance, most believe that the lessons of Prohibition are remembered. However, somehow, without prohibiting alcohol, ways must be found to reduce the toll caused by drinking alcohol.

Alcohol is a key factor in many fatal accidents, especially crashes involving drivers in their teens and early twenties.

Because of alcohol's widespread use, the alcohol industry is huge and politically powerful.

5 MONEY TO BE MADE

"The alcohol industry contends that its advertising is geared to encourage people to switch brands. They and the tobacco industry are the only two advertisers making such claims. In fact, their advertising for the most part is geared to recruit new young users."

Manocherian Foundation

Alcohol is a legal drug, by far the most commonly used drug in the world. Making and selling alcohol is a huge business in the United States. It is also a major source of tax dollars for the federal government, as well as for state and local governments.

Consider beer. In the United States it ranks fourth in consumption of *any* kind of beverage, behind soft drinks, milk, and coffee. Sales of beer in the mid-1990s were about $51 billion annually. This yielded several billion dollars of tax revenues. In a sense, governments are as dependent on alcohol taxes as an alcoholic is on his or her drug. Some people believe that this makes both federal and state governments reluctant to take actions needed to warn people about the dangers of alcohol.

Soon after its birth as a nation the United States began to tax alcohol. In 1791 Congress enacted an excise tax on distilled spirits. (Unlike a sales tax, which is collected at the time of sale, an excise tax is paid directly to the government by the manufacturer.) The distillers, then making whiskey mostly in western Pennsylvania, resisted the tax with violence. President George Washington had to send thousands of troops to put down what became known as the Whiskey Rebellion.

During the Whiskey Rebellion, federal officials who tried to collect taxes on whiskey were sometimes tarred and feathered.

Although that unpopular tax was repealed in 1802, others have since been established. In the mid-1990s, federal taxes represented about a quarter of the cost of a bottle of liquor. State and local taxes made up another 20 percent of the cost. On alcoholic beverages from

abroad, the federal government also charges import duties. Since the end of Prohibition in 1933, federal regulation of the alcohol industry has been under the domain of the Bureau of Alcohol, Tobacco and Firearms (BATF), part of the U.S. Department of the Treasury. Although the BATF sometimes shuts down illegal distilleries, its primary job is tax collection. The bureau monitors the financial records of distilleries, breweries, and wineries to ensure that the U.S. Treasury gets the correct amount of taxes.

Different kinds of drinks are taxed at different rates. Even though a can of beer, a glass of wine, and a shot of liquor contain roughly the same amount of alcohol, the federal excise tax rate on liquor is twice that on beer and three times that on wine. This inequality can be traced back to the belief that liquor is more harmful than beer or wine. Today, however, it can be argued that beer is the drink that is most costly to society, and that therefore it should be taxed the most heavily. Beer is the most popular alcoholic drink of teenagers and young men, and beer drinking is involved in many more accidents, crimes, and alcohol-related traffic accidents than liquor drinking.

Excise taxes on alcohol have not kept pace with inflation. For example, between l951 and 1991, Congress increased the federal tax on a bottle of liquor by 29 percent. During that forty-year span, however, consumer prices actually increased by 400 percent. If taxes had kept up with consumer prices, all alcoholic drinks would be much more expensive today.

That would be a good thing, according to people concerned about the deaths and other costs caused by alcohol. Sales of alcohol tend to fall when prices rise. This is especially true of liquor sales, but it applies to other drinks too. Although higher prices cause some drinkers merely to switch to cheaper brands in order to continue their usual alcohol intake, they cause many others to drink less.

This drop in alcohol consumption has good effects for society as a whole. One researcher studied thirty-nine instances in which states raised their liquor tax and found a decrease in the number of traffic fatalities in those states. A link between a rise in state liquor taxes and a drop in violent crime has also been found.

Any attempt to raise taxes on alcohol is opposed by the alcohol industry, which is a powerful lobbying force both in Congress and in state legislatures. Companies began to form trade associations to oppose tax increases more than a century ago. In 1862 the United States Brewers Association was organized. Members supported political candidates who were likely to vote for lower beer taxes. The taxes were lowered. Soon liquor distillers began to lobby Congress in an organized fashion as well.

Today the Distilled Spirits Council of the United States is the liquor industry's trade association. The Beer Institute works for the interests of brewers, and the Wine Institute represents the wine industry. For many decades producers of these three kinds of alcoholic drinks felt they were in competition for drinkers' dollars. To some extent they are, but the differences between producers have become somewhat blurred, as some liquor companies have purchased major wineries.

In 1992 the beer industry in the United States sold $51.3 billion of its product. Liquor makers sold $30.9 billion, wine makers $12.9

billion. The total was just over $95 billion. These were typical sales figures throughout the early to mid-1990s.

The alcohol industry employs more than three million people. Its needs also lead to jobs in many other enterprises, including retail liquor stores, glass and can manufacturing, advertising, and farming. Many farmers sell crops of corn, rye, barley, rice, and other grains to the alcohol industry. This is the agricultural output of

Barley seeds (left) are a basic ingredient of beer, while corn (right), rice, rye, and other grains are used to make liquors.

more than four million acres of farmland. The alcohol industry affects not just farmers but also businesses that sell equipment, fertilizers, and other farming supplies.

In addition to its far-reaching economic effects and its power to affect laws, the alcohol industry touches the lives of everyone through advertising. About $2 billion is spent annually to advertise alcoholic drinks and to promote them in other ways—for example, by sponsoring rock concerts. The cost of an advertising campaign for one brand of beer can be enormous. In 1993 Anheuser Busch spent $110 million on advertisements for its Budweiser brand beer.

Since Prohibition all kinds of alcoholic drinks have been advertised on billboards and in magazines, newspapers, and other print media. Beer and wine have also been advertised on radio and television. Until 1996, liquor had not been advertised on television and radio; then the liquor industry broke its own voluntary ban on such advertisements. The ban had been in effect since 1936 for radio and 1948 for television.

To many observers, it seemed that this decision by the Distilled Spirits Council was related to declining liquor sales. For nearly two decades, liquor consumption in the United States has been dropping. Meanwhile, beer and wine—still judged by the public to be less harmful than liquor—have been advertised on radio and television. Although the liquor industry denied being concerned about sales, spokespeople said liquor distillers were at a competitive disadvantage. They felt that the ban was obsolete.

This change brought a strong response from those concerned about drinking by young people. President Bill Clinton said the

Until 1996 the liquor industry advertised only in magazines and newspapers. This magazine ad seems to suggest that alcohol provides consumers with better friends.

move meant "exposing our children to such ads before they know how to handle alcohol or are legally allowed to do so…. To the liquor companies we should say, you were right for the last fifty years when you didn't advertise on television; you're wrong to change your policy now." The chairman of the Federal Communications Commission (FCC), Reed Hundt, said that the action by the distillers "is disappointing for parents, and dangerous for our kids."

Liquor ads began to appear on some cable television stations, particularly during telecasts of sports events. The four major television networks vowed not to carry liquor commercials, so many viewers saw no change. However, the end of the liquor industry's self-imposed ban sparked national debate about all advertising of alcohol and its effects on young people.

Legislation was introduced in Congress to ban liquor ads from the airwaves. Many legal experts believed this effort was doomed because it would violate the First Amendment to the Constitution, which protects free speech. Advertising is considered a form of speech. Banning liquor ads but not those of beer and wine would be unfair unless it could be shown that liquor was especially harmful to drinkers, and in particular underage drinkers.

Two agencies of the federal government have some say in the content of alcohol advertisements. The Federal Trade Commission (FTC) has the power to order an end to false or misleading advertisements. The BATF has rules against ads that are obscene or misleading, or that link drinking with athletic ability. The bureau ordered the maker of a drink called Cisco to change its packaging. Cisco is wine with alcohol added, which raises its alcohol content to about 20 percent, yet its packaging resembled that of wine coolers, which have a low alcohol content.

A third federal agency, the Food and Drug Administration (FDA), has no control over alcohol advertising. Some people believe it should have such jurisdiction, since alcohol is a legal drug. With other legal, pharmaceutical drugs, FDA rules ensure that consumers get information about both benefits and risks. As things stand now, alcohol advertisements show and tell only about social and psychological benefits—real or imagined. The sole exception is the brief warning in tiny print about the possibility of birth defects and other risks that has been required on containers of alcoholic beverages since 1989. It is up to parents, schools, public health agencies, and private groups concerned about alcohol abuse to warn consumers of the risks.

In its defense, the alcohol industry points to its advertisements that urge drinkers to "drink safely" or to "know when to say when." These moderation messages, as they are called, were criticized by Patricia Taylor of the Center for Science in the Public Interest, during her testimony before a Congressional subcommittee in 1990. She said, "Have you thought about what Spuds McKenzie [a dog character used in beer commercials in the 1980s] telling your ten-year-old to 'Know When To Say When' really means? First, your child is getting a pro-drinking message. 'Know When To Say When' assumes that someone has started drinking, and the only question that needs to be answered is, how much? There certainly is no information about the fact that it is illegal for your ten-year-old to purchase alcoholic beverages before reaching the age of twenty-one, or

"You can still get hammered for cheap" and start drinking at breakfast, suggest these ads aimed at college students.

that alcohol is a drug or that alcohol can be deadly.... The American public deserves and needs more than a subtle pro-drinking message in sheep's clothing from beer barons worried that the public is catching on to the fact that their product is America's leading drug problem."

The alcohol industry does do some self-policing of its advertisements. For example, the Beer Institute publishes an Advertising and Marketing Code that lists rules aimed at limiting exposure of people under twenty-one to beer ads or marketing events. The rules include using actors or models at least twenty-five years old, and not depicting Santa Claus in advertisements. However, most of the rules are loose enough to allow ads and other marketing promotions that appeal strongly to underage drinkers. Dr. Charles Rongey wrote in *The Encyclopedia of Drugs and Alcohol,* "The beer industry's voluntary advertising codes are vaguely or narrowly written so as to restrict advertising practices as little as possible."

Since the mid-1980s the legal drinking age in all fifty states has been twenty-one. It is illegal for anyone aged twenty or younger to buy alcoholic drinks. The challenge to the alcohol industry is to promote its products to people twenty-one or older but not to those who are underage. The industry claims that is its goal, but many of its advertisements and promotions suggest otherwise. Each year, for example, beer companies spend about $20 million promoting their products on college campuses and at college spring break gathering places. Ads for alcoholic beverages account for about 35 percent of the advertising income of college newspapers. Wherever college students gather, alcohol distributors and bars team up to offer all-you-can-drink specials.

The alcohol industry claims that it advertises to encourage people of legal drinking age to switch brands. If this is true, why promote drinking to college students, many of whom are not yet twenty-one? More likely, this multimillion-dollar effort is aimed at recruiting new customers. There's money to be made. A college freshman lured into an allegiance to a brand of beer will spend $50,000 (with the effects of inflation figured in) on that beer alone in a lifetime.

George Hacker, executive director of the Center for Science in the Public Interest, said, "Kids don't usually wait to start drinking when they're twenty-one in this country. And they also don't start opening their eyes to advertising until they are twenty-one years of age."

In reality, people see plenty of ads, particularly beer ads on television, long before age twenty-one. They see advertisements for alcohol when they are teenagers, when they are kindergartners, when they are toddlers. A 1995 study found that 73 percent of children nine to eleven years old recognized frogs as television characters promoting Budweiser beer. Television ads for beer convey the ideas that alcohol is a source of pleasure, a key to having fun, and a way to become more attractive to the opposite sex and to have a successful social life. Drinking, it seems, is an answer in life's major questions: happiness, friendship, success, attractiveness, and sex.

Teenagers are just as concerned about life's major questions as are adults of legal drinking age—perhaps *more* concerned. Usually

Animals and humorous situations that appeal to children are often featured in beer advertisements.

they feel eager to become adults, to become independent, to do adult things. Their inexperience and lack of information about all aspects of drinking make them especially vulnerable to the messages in countless advertisements for alcohol. So the alcohol industry, in need of new customers, finds plenty of young recruits.

Through its advertising and other promotions, the alcohol industry is the primary educator of the public about alcohol. The amount it spends on advertising dwarfs information from groups and individuals concerned about alcohol's health and safety issues.

These concerned groups and individuals keep trying to make the playing field more level. Beginning in the mid-1980s, laws have been introduced in Congress to require equal time on television and radio for health and safety messages about drinking. The alcohol industry has been successful in keeping this legislation from coming to a vote in Congress. Similar equal-time messages about tobacco were effective and caused a decline in smoking. They were so effective, in fact, that the tobacco industry was actually pleased to be barred from television and radio advertising in 1971.

Beginning in 1990 legislation has also been introduced in Congress to require several health and safety messages on all alcohol advertising. The messages, five to seven in number, used on a rotating schedule, would be like the warnings required on ads and packages for tobacco products. Two examples are "SURGEON GENERAL'S WARNING: Alcohol is a drug and may be addictive," and "SURGEON GENERAL'S WARNING: If you drink too much alcohol too fast, you can die of alcohol poisoning."

One sponsor of this legislation was Senator Strom Thurmond, Republican of South Carolina, whose daughter, Nancy Moore Thurmond, was run down and killed by a drunk driver in 1993. This legislation has been introduced in each new session of Congress, but so far the lobbying efforts of the alcohol industry and its allies—especially the advertising industry—have kept it from becoming law.

Another proposed law would phase out all television and radio advertising of all kinds of alcohol over a ten-year period. This proposal is promoted strongly by the Manocherian Foundation, whose founder and president lost two friends to an impaired driver when he was a high school student. In its pamphlets and videos, the Manocherian Foundation points out a major inconsistency in the position of the U.S. government regarding alcohol and other drugs:

> If a person is caught with an ounce of marijuana, he is arrested, prosecuted, and incarcerated. Marijuana and other illegal drugs cause six thousand deaths per year. On the other hand, our government allows $2 billion annually worth of promotions and advertising so that the alcohol industry can sell some $92 billion per year of the drug known as ALCOHOL. Does it make sense for our government to allow the promotion of one drug that costs society 100,000 deaths and $100 billion each year, while the same government spends billions to stop the use and distribution of other drugs? We do not believe so.

The Manocherian Foundation does not seek prohibition or abstinence from drinking by adults. It argues that the alcohol industry should not be free to promote a drug that affects the population much more adversely than all illegal drugs combined. It urges that the industry's role as chief educator about alcohol—through its advertising—should be stopped.

France now prohibits all alcohol advertising on radio, television, and billboards. Achieving this in the United States would be very difficult, given the political power of the alcohol industry and its allies. However, the airwaves used by television and radio are owned by the public and are supposed to be regulated in the public interest by the Federal Communications Commission (FCC). Clearly, it is not in

the public interest to continue to allow the alcohol industry to "teach" everyone, especially young people, that their products are a trouble-free answer to life's problems.

In its video called "Sex, Lies and Profits," the Manocherian Foundation analyzes the messages in alcohol ads and questions why a drug that causes so much harm should be freely advertised.

6 A SPECIAL RISK FOR YOUNG PEOPLE

"Our health message is clear. The use of alcohol by young people can lead to serious health consequences far beyond those well known about drinking and driving—the likes of absenteeism, vandalism, date rape, truancy, theft, and random violence, to name a few. But that message directly conflicts with the enticing drumbeat of ads that say drink me and you will be cool, drink me and you will be glamorous, or drink me and you will have fun."

Antonia Novello, former Surgeon General of the United States

Alcohol is a poison and a drug, and its abuse causes untold suffering. Most observers agree, however, that moderate drinking by responsible adults is not harmful. In fact, there is evidence that taking small amounts can be beneficial. Several studies have shown that people who never drink have a higher risk for heart attacks than people who drink moderate amounts of alcohol (especially red wine). Moderate drinking also helps lower levels of cholesterol and prevent colds, unless the drinker smokes tobacco. Research in the United States, England, and several other nations has confirmed these benefits of drinking.

So far, however, no research has defined the optimal amount of alcohol to drink, the amount that would help reduce the risk of heart attacks but do no harm. The dietary guidelines of the U.S. government state that "one or two drinks daily appear to cause no harm to adults." However, the American Cancer Society declared in 1996 that "cancer risk increases with the amount of alcohol consumed and may start to rise with intake of as few as two drinks a day."

Two drinks a day would be 24 ounces of beer, 10 ounces of wine, or 3 ounces of 80-proof liquor. Many would call this moderate drinking, but this term means different things to different people. According to some liquor advertisements, moderate drinking is four drinks a day! Most adults consider one or two drinks a day a moderate amount. For women, who usually weigh less than men, no more than one drink a day is generally agreed to represent moderate drinking. Millions of people drink far more. In fact, if every single adult in the United States had two drinks a day, the alcohol industry would lose 40 percent of its income.

The whole concept of moderate drinking has to be discarded, however, when the drinker is underage. What may be moderate for an adult is often excessive for a teenager. At any age alcohol impairs judgment and the senses and can encourage reckless driving and other risky behavior. But teenagers are more likely to be harmed than adults, for several reasons. The most basic is size. Because teenagers usually weigh less than adults, a given amount of alcohol is more likely to impair or intoxicate them, or—after downing several drinks in a short time—kill them.

A beginning drinker of any age has to learn about his or her re-

sponse to alcohol. Because of weight and metabolism, among other factors, each individual's response is unique. Whether the person has eaten or is tired can also influence the effects of alcohol. Young drinkers are often surprised to learn how little alcohol it takes to seriously impair their senses. So a lack of experience with alcohol is also part of the special risk for teenagers.

In addition to lacking knowledge of their own response to alco-

Each person responds to alcohol differently, and teenagers are especially vulnerable to the effects of this drug.

1 to 2 Drinks

Drivers ages 16 to 19 with a blood alcohol concentration (BAC) of .02% to .05%—that's only one to two drinks—are

7 TIMES

more likely to be killed in a crash than a sober driver of any age group.

3 to 4 Drinks

With three or four drinks (BAC of .085%), young drivers are

40 TIMES

more likely to be killed than a sober driver and 20 times more likely to be killed than a 55-year-old driver with the same BAC.

4 to 6 Drinks

By four to six drinks (BAC of .12%), teenagers are

90 TIMES

more likely to die in a crash than a sober driver.

Teenagers are at greater risk than adults of dying in a car crash, partly because of alcohol's stronger effects on lighter people.

Source: American Automobile Association (AAA)

hol, many young people lack basic information about what they drink. This was learned in a nationwide survey conducted in 1991 by the U.S. Department of Health and Human Services. Interviewers asked questions of a large sample of students in order to learn about the knowledge and drinking habits of the nation's 20.7 million seventh through twelfth graders. They discovered that many students lacked essential knowledge about alcohol and its effects. More than a third of the teenagers believed that fresh air, a cold shower, or drinking coffee would "sober up" a drunk person. Almost 80 percent of the students did not know that a shot of whiskey has the same amount of alcohol as 12 ounces of beer. About a third did not know that all wine coolers contain alcohol.

Even when they had read the labels on cans and bottles, many teenagers were confused about the alcohol content of various drinks—due in part to the lack of clarity on the containers. This was especially true of so-called wine coolers, a favorite of beginning drinkers. According to this study, junior and senior high school students drink 35 percent of all wine coolers sold in the United States. More than a third of the students did not know that Cisco contains alcohol. Even after being told that it is 20 percent alcohol, more than 25 percent of the teenagers believed that beer or malt liquor contained more alcohol than Cisco. (Beer contains between 3 and 8 percent alcohol; malt liquor, between 5.6 and 10.9 percent.)

Many of the students who were interviewed said they obtained their information about alcohol and drinking from friends, "just picked it up," or learned from the media. Of course "the media" includes advertisements paid for by the alcohol industry. Students

Small, hard-to-read labels contribute to the ignorance of people about the content of alcohol beverages.

who were nondrinkers were much more likely to learn about alcohol from their family and school than were students who drank.

Additionally, the survey found that millions of teenagers are also unsure about the legal age to buy alcohol (now twenty-one in all states). There was no doubt, however, that those who wanted to drink could get alcohol. Many teenagers reported that they got drinks from friends, at parties, or in their own homes, with or without their parents' knowledge. Many state health officials concerned about teenage drinking agree that a number of kids are encouraged to drink by lax parental behavior.

Despite state minimum age laws, students as young as twelve or thirteen said they could buy alcohol in stores. Seven million students buy their alcohol from stores and say it is usually easy to obtain. They find stores known to sell alcohol to minors, or young cashiers who are often willing to sell to an underage buyer. Forty-four states allow minors to sell alcohol without adult supervision, and an estimated three million students buy alcohol where they know the cashier.

Teenagers also use fake identification cards, which are easily obtained. One state official said that minors attempt to buy alcohol no matter how poor the identification. He cited a case in which a vendor was charged with selling beer to a minor: "The vendor asked for

Teenagers report that it is easy to obtain cards identifying them as adults.

ID. The sixteen-year-old boy—who looked sixteen—presented an ID of a five-foot four-inch female, except that he had taped his picture on it. He was a six-foot five-inch male. Nonetheless, the clerk sold beer to him. Luckily, our officers had the store under surveillance and saw him carrying the beer out."

State laws against underage drinking are not strongly enforced. Courts are usually lenient, with most penalties not strong deterrents. A state official said, "The one thing that a minor cares about is his driver's license. Other penalties do not work." Twenty-seven states delay, suspend, or revoke youth drivers' licenses for some alcohol-related violations.

In addition to ready availability of alcohol and the lack of accurate information about drinking and alcohol, teenagers are at special risk simply because they are teenagers. Adolescence is a time of many new experiences and of mastering new skills. For most teens, driving is one of those skills. Yet it is another aspect of life where lack of experience can hurt. Teenagers are also more likely than adults to engage in risky behavior. At times they feel invincible. Combining this attitude with alcohol, or other drugs, and inexperience can have serious or even fatal consequences.

In 1996, 17,274 people in the United States died in alcohol-related traffic crashes. Of these, nearly twenty-five hundred were between the ages of sixteen and twenty. The number one killer of fifteen- to twenty-four-year-olds is alcohol-related auto crashes. Traffic deaths are especially high at times when people often drink to excess—Super Bowl Sunday, Saint Patrick's Day, the early morning hours following New Year's Eve—but also on spring weekends

Alcohol-related vehicle crashes are the number one killer of fifteen- to twenty-four-year-olds in the United States.

when proms and graduations occur. Fatalities are, of course, only part of the story. Many thousands of young drivers, passengers, and pedestrians are also injured, sometimes handicapped for life, in accidents caused by drinking.

It has been calculated that *every day* in the United States 427 teens are arrested for alcohol abuse or driving while intoxicated. Annually about two million people are arrested for drunk driving. Law enforcement officials know that this is only a small fraction of all violators. The chance of being caught when driving drunk is quite small.

People who drive drunk are likely to be heavy drinkers with a serious alcohol problem. They make up about half of all people arrested for drunk driving. Statistically, however, they are greatly outnumbered on the highways by light to moderate alcohol drinkers, some of whom occasionally drink heavily or do some binge drinking.

Binge drinking—consuming five or more drinks in a row or in a short time span—is a major problem for high school and college students today. Several million teenagers binge at least once a month. (The range is from one to twenty binges in a month.) According to one national study, a typical binge drinker is a sixteen-year-old male in the tenth grade who took his first drink when he was twelve. He usually consumes six drinks a week. Less typical is a group of almost a half million students in eleventh grade who average fifteen drinks weekly and binge almost every week. Although most binge drinking occurs in high school and college, a 1993 survey found that 14 percent of eighth graders said they had had five or more drinks in a row on at least one occasion in the prior two weeks.

The goal of binge drinking is to get drunk. A high school senior in Minnesota said, "Kids at my high school drink not because they enjoy it, but because they think it's cool. It's status to say, 'Hey, I got drunk last night.'"

By overwhelming their bodies' defenses against alcohol, binge drinkers may die of alcohol poisoning or suffocate after vomiting while unconscious (see page 29). Between 1991 and 1995, admissions to emergency rooms for alcohol poisoning jumped 15 percent in college communities. Some binge drinkers die from strokes, as the overdose of alcohol reduces the flow of blood to their brains.

Among high school students, those who binge almost every week are usually boys (87 percent males, 13 percent females). But among those who binge less frequently, 41 percent are female, and binge drinking is common among college-age women. In 1992, Dr. Robert Cloninger, who studies the causes of alcoholism, wrote, "It's becoming more socially acceptable for young women to drink as heavily as only their fathers would have in a previous generation. With this social change we are going to be seeing more women alcoholics."

In 1993, nearly 10 percent (over 110,000) of the people admitted to state-funded alcohol-treatment programs were under age twenty-one. Although children as young as nine have been diagnosed as alcoholics, it usually takes several years for alcoholism to develop. Youngsters with drinking problems are more accurately called potential alcoholics. Minors typically begin to drink at age twelve or thirteen. Many of them drink for reasons that can lead to serious drinking problems and alcoholism. They drink to help cope with certain feelings—for example, to avoid boredom or to ease being upset. Many of them also drink alone. This behavior can be an early step toward dependence on alcohol. Of course, anyone can become an alcoholic, but those at greatest risk are the seven million children below the age of eighteen whose families include adult alcoholics.

In most communities there are sources of help for people of any age who recognize that they have a drinking problem (see pages 95–102). An obstacle for most people is admitting that they have a problem and need help. This obstacle is especially huge for teenagers, who often need to feel independent and in control of their own lives.

There are many groups and individuals at work trying to reduce the terrible toll of the drug alcohol in the United States. Some are groups of young people who offer advice to their peers or raise questions about common notions concerning drinking. Varsity Athletes Against Substance Abuse is one such group.

Another is Students Against Driving Drunk (SADD), which focuses on the problem of drunk driving by students. Formed in 1981, SADD has chapters in high schools in every state. Although school-based (and now including middle schools as well as high schools), SADD also reaches out to families and communities in its educational programs. It offers plans for alcohol-free parties at prom and graduation times. It encourages teenagers to sign a "prom pledge"— a promise not to drink or use drugs on prom night.

SADD also encourages teenagers and their parents to sign a "Contract for Life." The student agrees to call a parent if he or she has been drinking or if the person responsible for driving has been drinking. The parent, in turn, pledges to provide a ride home. This contract drew some criticism because it seemed to some to communicate that drinking itself was not a problem, as long as drunk driving was avoided.

The same criticism has been aimed at the concept of the "designated driver"—one person who does not drink and is sober, allowing his or her passengers to drink but have safe transportation. The Office of Substance Abuse Prevention (part of the Department of Health and Human Services), which evaluates alcohol and drug

Students Against Driving Drunk (SADD) has chapters in high schools in every state and promotes alcohol-free parties for teenagers.

information intended for use in schools, said in 1993: "Materials recommending a designated driver should be rated unacceptable. They encourage heavy alcohol use by implying it is okay to drink to intoxication as long as you don't drive."

Defending its "Contract for Life," SADD has stated, "The 'Contract for Life' does not condone or permit teen drinking. It does acknowledge that teens may find themselves in dangerous situations. By facilitating family communication before a dangerous situation occurs, the 'Contract for Life' saves lives and helps bring and keep families together."

The Office of Substance Abuse Prevention (now called the Center for Substance Abuse Prevention) also issues guidelines to media, encouraging new ways of describing drug and alcohol use. The office suggested, for example, that instead of referring to "responsible use" of alcohol, newspapers and magazines should refer just to "use, since there is a risk associated with all use."

Whether this way of thinking applies to adults can be argued, but it certainly pertains to minors. As explored in the first half of this chapter, the idea of moderate (or "responsible") drinking does not really apply to teenagers. Further reasons were explained in the November 1995 issue of *On the Move,* the newsletter of SADD:

> There's no such thing as responsible underage drinking.... It is illegal for anyone under the age of twenty-one to drink; like all crimes, getting caught drinking under the age of twenty-one can lead to arrest, a fine, loss of license, and even a criminal record.... Beyond that the use of alcohol interferes with a person's judgment and reflexes, breaks down inhibitions, and gives people a false sense of confidence, causing them to do things they normally wouldn't; later to regret that action. Teenagers who drink too much are more likely to get pregnant or suffer sexually transmitted diseases, such as AIDS.
>
> The use of alcohol by teenagers is a common thread in a majority of suicides, date rapes, violence, drownings, and boat accidents. Is a few hours of fun worth any of these?... Alcohol in any amount doesn't make you smarter, sexier, or healthier. Usually all drinking does is make you smell, act stupid, and hurt yourself and others.... Responsible drinking? No such thing!

About the time SADD was formed, two other national organizations began to fight for tough drunk-driving laws. One was Remove

As state drunk-driving laws have been toughened, more and more young alcohol abusers are sentenced to work camps or prisons.

Intoxicated Drivers (RID-USA); the other, Mothers Against Drunk Driving (MADD). Many members were victims or surviving family members of drunk-driving tragedies. Both groups have persuaded state legislatures to pass laws that provide for prison terms, license suspension, educational classes for people convicted of driving drunk, and other actions aimed to reduce drunk-driving offenses.

The number of deaths from drunk driving declined annually from 1986 to 1995, but rose 4 percent (to 17,274) in 1996. MADD and RID-USA continue to call for stricter laws, including tougher

Family photos of victims send a powerful message against letting drunks drive, as can be seen in this advertisement sponsored by the U.S. Department of Transportation and the Advertising Council.

The DeLair Family
Trish, Kevin, Jen & Jon Jon
The family that played and stayed together,
were killed by a drunk driver together.
June 6, 1992, Butler, PA

If you don't stop someone from driving drunk, who will? Do whatever it takes.

FRIENDS DON'T LET FRIENDS DRIVE DRUNK.

Ad Council

U.S. Department of Transportation

penalties for first-time offenders. Those arrested once for drunk driving—including many teenagers—often drive drunk again. Between a quarter and a third of drivers involved in fatal crashes have prior arrests for drunk driving.

Another goal of MADD and RID-USA is to lower the definition of intoxication to a blood alcohol concentration (BAC) of .08 percent. Fourteen states have adopted this limit; thirty-six use the more lenient BAC standard of .10 percent. Both organizations point out that a BAC as low as .05 percent is known to impair driving ability— according to MADD, hundreds of lives would be saved each year if all states used the .08 standard. However, this is opposed by the alcohol, restaurant, and bar industries. In 1996 these business interests spent large sums of money lobbying in eleven states whose legislatures were voting on this matter. Laws to adopt the .08 standard were defeated in all eleven states.

On the issues of drunk driving, underage drinking, and other problems involving its products, the alcohol industry prefers running advertisements urging people to "Know When To Say When." It remains for others—individuals, families, concerned organizations—to look elsewhere for solutions to the number one drug abuse problem in the United States.

Part of the solution lies in asking questions about the widespread acceptance of alcohol in everyday life. It lies in asking questions about a society that makes light of drunkenness in films and on television, a society that does not question the underlying messages on T-shirts that say "College: A Bar with a $20,000 Cover Charge" or "Drink Till He's Cute." It lies in asking questions about the notions

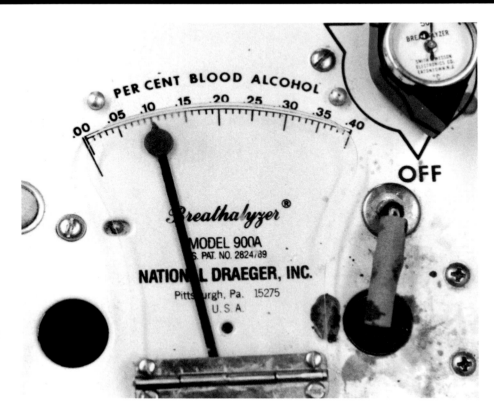

A Breathalyzer measures the concentration of alcohol in a person's exhaled breath, an indicator of his or her blood alcohol concentration (BAC).

advanced in the thousands of alcohol advertisements everyone—including children—sees each year.

And part of the solution to the nation's number one drug problem lies in questions young people ask of themselves—about their own lives and the choices they make when it comes to alcohol. The answers will surely have a profound effect on their future.

GETTING HELP WITH DRINKING PROBLEMS

There is a wealth of treatment programs for alcoholism and other drinking problems, but the problems themselves can be avoided if the dangers of the drug are recognized early and dealt with cautiously. Millions of people simply choose not to drink. Some religions, including the Mormon and Muslim faiths, forbid drinking. As a result, in heavily Mormon Utah the incidence of alcoholism and of drunk driving is very low. Also, in some religious groups or in individual families, young people pledge to put off drinking until at least twenty-one, the legal drinking age.

This may seem crazy or stupid to some teenagers who have started drinking or who have friends who drink. They may feel those who don't drink are really missing something. By age eighteen the average person in the United States has been exposed to seventy-five thousand beer advertisements on television. These ads teach that alcohol is a normal and even essential part of life. Nevertheless, nondrinkers get along fine without alcohol.

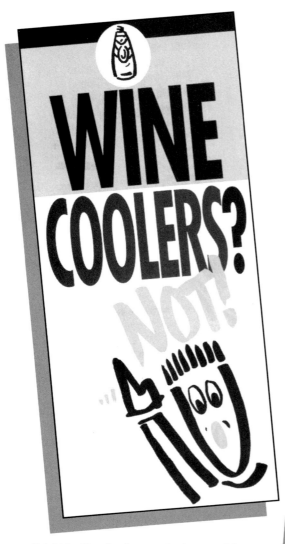

Helpful booklets, brochures, and other materials are available for teenagers or their families who are seeking information about alcohol and choices about drinking.

Before deciding whether to drink or when to start, a person ought to read the results of studies in which young men and women thought they were consuming alcohol but weren't. This research is described in detail in Alan Lang's *Alcohol: Teenage Drinking (The Encyclopedia of Psychoactive Drugs)*. The studies involved volunteers in different social situations. Some were served alcoholic drinks, others were not, but in both groups some individuals were misinformed about what they were drinking. In one study, male college students who *believed* they were drinking alcohol but were not reported that the drinks they had consumed made them feel less anxious when they were instructed to try to make a good impression on a young woman. Conclusion: "Just the belief that they had consumed alcohol was enough to reduce their social anxiety."

In another study, young women who consumed alcohol or just *believed* they had actually felt more anxious in a social situation—trying to make a good impression on an unfamiliar man. Researchers believed that the women may have feared the man's disapproval of their drinking or feared being intoxicated in an unfamiliar situation. The conclusion of this and other studies is that society has taught us to feel a certain way when we drink—or believe we drink—alcohol. People probably have much more control over their behavior in social situations than they think. Alcohol is not the essential "social lubricant" that many believe.

Nevertheless, sometimes the pressure to begin drinking, or to drink heavily, can be very strong. In some schools students learn ways to fight this pressure—for example, by practicing refusal skills. Saying no often takes courage, and it helps to have some ready answers. Several are provided in "Saying 'NO'" (on page 102), which is reprinted from the December 1996 issue of *On the Move,* the high school newsletter of Students Against Driving Drunk (SADD).

Knowledge can be a powerful weapon against drinking problems. Everyone is taught some ideas about alcohol by the advertisements of the alcohol industry. The truth about alcohol and its effects has to come from other sources. There are plenty of booklets, newsletters, videos, posters, and other materials available— often free—from the organizations listed on pages 103–4. Helpful information may also be available locally, from public health agencies or chapters of national groups (SADD and MADD, for example).

Young people who feel they may have a drinking problem or who are concerned about a friend's or a parent's drinking can also find help. Effective treatments are available for alcoholism and other drinking problems, though no single treatment works for everyone. For any treatment to help, however, the drinker first has to admit he or she has a problem.

This is no small challenge. In self-defense, many people tend to think of the most dramatic drunken behavior as evidence of a drinking problem. Everything else is just social drinking. As the author Elizabeth Ryan points out in her book *Straight Talk about Drugs and Alcohol,* this black-and-white view makes it easier for people to dismiss the troubling thought that they might have a drinking problem.

Elizabeth Ryan suggests a more helpful and realistic way of looking at drinking: as a spectrum or range of situations. At one end are light drinkers; at the other, people who are alcoholics or people with drinking problems that seriously impair their work and home life.

In between there is a range of different situations. They include people who go on occasional binges or who feel they cannot have a good time at a party without alcohol. At times such people may say to themselves, "Maybe I have a drinking problem."

Such organizations as Alcoholics Anonymous have devised lists of questions that help people judge whether they (or a friend or family member) have a drinking problem. Some lists include twenty or more questions. Here are ten especially important ones:

1. Do you lose time from school because of drinking?
2. Do you drink to build your self-confidence?
3. Do you drink alone?
4. Do you have to have a drink when you go to a party or on a date?
5. Do you drink to escape from worries?
6. Do you get into financial troubles over buying alcohol?
7. Do your friends drink less than you?
8. Do you often think and talk about drinking?
9. Do you find yourself hanging out mostly with people who drink alcohol?
10. Do you find yourself having accidents or have you gotten into trouble with police or other authorities as a result of drinking?

According to researchers who have studied alcoholism, a "yes" answer to just one of these questions is a warning that the drinker may be becoming an alcoholic. The more "yes" answers, the more serious the drinking problem.

Some of the above questions can be useful when a young person thinks one or both parents may have a drinking problem. Here are other, more specific questions about parents:

1. Do either or both parents have alcohol on their breath before lunch?
2. Do either or both parents gulp down alcoholic drinks?
3. Do either or both parents ever get drunk on working days?
4. Do either or both parents, once they start drinking, always continue until they are drunk?
5. Do either or both parents hide bottles of alcohol?
6. Do either or both parents sometimes stay intoxicated for several days?
7. Do either or both parents ever injure themselves or others while drinking?

A "yes" to three or more of these questions suggests strongly that the drinking parent or parents may be alcoholics. Any teenager in this situation should seek support and guidance. Help may be available from a family doctor, school counselor, member of the clergy, or community social worker. One well-known source is Alateen (address on page 103), a national group for anyone between ages thirteen and nineteen who has an alcoholic parent or relative. It is associated with Al-Anon, which helps families and friends of alcoholics. There are many local branches of Alateen, whose goal is to help teenagers deal with the problem of living in an alcoholic home.

In a growing number of homes, it is not the parents but a teenager who is the alcoholic. Although most alcoholics are adults, Alcoholics Anonymous now has groups for teenagers in many cities and smaller communities. This self-help organization, often called just AA, has about two million members in thousands of groups. People who are trying to control their drinking problem give one another support and advice.

Several of AA's twelve steps, and its basic credo, refer to God. This religious aspect of AA makes some people uncomfortable. In 1987 Jack Trimpey founded a group called Rational Recovery (RR), which treats alcoholism and other addictions in a different way. This approach has grown in popularity, and RR discussion groups can be found in many cities.

No single program or treatment is effective for every drinker. Some people are helped by psychological counseling. Some benefit from the use of Antabuse, a drug that is taken several times a day. After taking Antabuse, a person suffers from nausea and powerful headaches if he or she drinks. This is a powerful incentive to give up alcohol. However, reliance on this drug alone does not get at the root of a person's drinking problem.

It is important for young people in particular to know that help is available, often in their own school or community, when they confront their drinking problem or those of friends or family members.

SAYING "NO"

Okay, so you know it's illegal and unsafe to use alcohol and other drugs, but how do you say "no" when someone is in your face, pressuring you?

Before you try to come up with a response, come up with an attitude—not a bad attitude, just a state of mind in which you believe you have a right to your own decisions and you owe no one an explanation. After all, if you said "yes" you wouldn't be asked for a reason. Why should you have to give a reason for saying "no"?

Once your attitude is in order, think of the simplest polite response you could make. "No thanks" is remarkably effective.

If a person doesn't accept your answer, don't feel obligated to give an explanation. Instead you might ask a question: "Why is it so important to you to make me take a drink?" This takes the pressure off of you and puts it on the other person. You don't have to discuss it. A person who has been drinking may be quick to argue, but you don't have to. Just maintain this attitude: No one else has the right to make me do something risky.

Sometimes it is easier to make a joke out of a peer pressure situation. Some SADD members have told us of success with lines like "No thanks, I can see the floor from here" or "I'm afraid it will ruin my figure."

"It makes me puke" will likely get you off the hook.

A simple factual response can also end the conversation. "I don't drink" is a great way to sum it up.

If you used to drink or use drugs, it's fine to say, "I got smart—I quit." If someone does not accept and respect your response, they have a problem—not you.

If you have trouble sticking up for yourself or standing by your answer, here is a trick you can use while you work on building up your confidence. Pick a person you trust and respect. Promise that person you will not drink or use drugs. Put it in writing if that will help you stand by it. Then, if anyone asks you to drink or use drugs, you can say, "I made a promise that I wouldn't—don't ask me to break my promise."

Finally, give some thought to where you go and who you go with. It isn't always possible to know if there will be alcohol and other drugs at a party, but a few questions and some advance planning can help you avoid situations where dangerous stuff can happen. Remember, you don't have to be drinking or drugging to be at risk. Sometimes the best way to say "no" is to be somewhere else.

Source: SADD, *On the Move*, December 1996.

SOURCES OF HELPFUL INFORMATION

The organizations marked with an asterisk (*) have programs or self-help materials for people who have drinking problems. Most provide free brochures and other materials. Some have books, videos, and other materials that can be ordered for a fee.

AAA Foundation for Traffic Safety, 1440 New York Avenue NW, Suite 201, Washington, DC 20005; (202) 638-5944

* Alateen and Al-Anon, Al-Anon Family Group Headquarters, 1600 Corporate Landing Parkway, Virginia Beach, VA 23454; (757) 563-1600

* Alcoholics Anonymous, P.O. Box 459, Grand Central Station, New York, NY 10163; (212) 870-3400

American Council on Alcoholism, White Marsh Business Center, 5024 Campbell Boulevard, Suite H, Baltimore, MD 21236; (800) 527-5344

Center for Science in the Public Interest, 1875 Connecticut Avenue NW, Washington, DC 20009; (202) 332-9110

Children of Alcoholics Foundation, P.O. Box 4185, Grand Central Station, New York, NY 10163; (800) 359-2623

* Hazelden Educational Materials, P.O. Box 176, Center City, MN 55012; (800) 328-9000

Manocherian Foundation, 3 New York Plaza, 18th floor, New York, NY 10004; (212) 837-4844

Mothers Against Drunk Driving (MADD), 511 East John Carpenter Freeway, Suite 700, Irving, TX 75062; (214) 744-6233

National Clearinghouse for Alcohol and Drug Information, P.O. Box 2345, Rockville, MD 20847; (800) 729-6686

* National Council on Alcoholism and Drug Dependence, 1511 K Street NW, Washington, DC 20005; (800) 622-2255

* Rational Recovery, P.O. Box 800, Lotus, CA 95651; (800) 303-2873

Remove Intoxicated Drivers (RID-USA), P.O. Box 520, Schenectady, NY 12301; (518) 393-HELP

Students Against Driving Drunk (SADD), P.O. Box 800, Marlborough, MA 01752; (508) 481-3568

GLOSSARY

alcohol—although there are several alcohol compounds, the one commonly consumed by people is ethyl alcohol, or ethanol. Small amounts of this poison slow the workings of the nervous system, producing pleasant, relaxed feelings. Larger amounts cause drunkenness and even death. Ethanol is the world's most widely used drug.

alcoholism—a chronic condition usually caused by excessive drinking of alcohol. A person who is an alcoholic is addicted to the drug and suffers unpleasant withdrawal symptoms when deprived of it.

binge drinking—consuming five or more alcoholic drinks in a row or in a short time. Since the liver cannot rid the body of alcohol quickly, binge drinking produces a high concentration of alcohol in the blood, causing severe drunkenness and even death.

blackout—the condition of being unable to remember what one said or did while intoxicated with alcohol.

blood alcohol concentration (BAC)—the amount of alcohol in the bloodstream. The percent of alcohol measured is a good gauge of a person's intoxication, and BAC levels are used in enforcement of laws against drunk driving.

cancer—a disorder in which body cells grow wildly, producing colonies called tumors, or neoplasms. Benign tumors are made up of cells similar to the surrounding tissues and are usually confined to one area. Malignant tumors are made up of cells unlike those nearby and tend to spread through the body. Cancer is the second leading cause of death in the United States.

cirrhosis—a serious liver condition usually caused by excessive drinking. Alcohol kills liver cells, producing scarred tissue that cannot effectively remove alcohol or other poisons from the body.

delerium tremens (DTs)—extreme withdrawal symptoms from alcohol, including trembling, sweating, nausea, confused feelings, and hallucinations.

distillation—a process in which alcohol is separated from fermenting juices of fruits, grains, or vegetables, producing a liquid (called liquor or distilled spirits) with a high alcohol content.

ethanol (ethyl alcohol)—see *alcohol*.

fermentation—the process in which yeast digests sugars in fruits, grains, or vegetables, producing alcohol and carbon dioxide. At one stage or another, all kinds of alcoholic drinks depend on the fermentation process.

fetal alcohol syndrome—physical and mental abnormalities in children born to women who drank alcohol while pregnant. The most severe damage usually occurs as a result of heavy drinking, but moderate amounts consumed at critical early stages of fetal development may also do harm.

fetus—an unborn human or other vertebrate that is more fully developed than an embryo. An unborn human reaches the fetus stage after two months in its mother's womb and is called a fetus until its moment of birth.

hangover—headache, nausea, and other unpleasant feelings experienced after having drunk alcohol to excess. These symptoms occur when alcohol causes swelling of blood vessels in the brain. The only cure is time—the amount of time needed for a person's liver to remove all alcohol from the blood.

hypertension—chronic high blood pressure, a condition often caused by heavy consumption of alcohol.

lobbying—trying to influence legislators and thereby the laws they produce. Sometimes lobbyists urge a legislator to propose a law or strengthen it with amendments while lobbyists representing other interests try to weaken it or persuade legislators to vote against the law.

Prohibition—the period from 1919 to 1933 when the U.S. government outlawed the making, transporting, and selling of liquor.

temperance—total abstinence from alcoholic drinks. The temperance movement in the United States first campaigned for moderation in drinking but eventually urged people to avoid alcohol entirely.

FURTHER READING

Claypool, Jane. *Alcohol and You.* New York: Franklin Watts, 1988.

David, Jay, editor. *The Family Secret: Adult Children of Alcoholics Tell Their Stories.* New York: William Morrow, 1994.

Diamond, Arthur. *Alcoholism.* San Diego: Lucent Books, 1992.

Emsley, John. "A Dispassionate Look at Alcohol." *Consumers' Research,* July 1995: 19–24.

Jaffe, Jerome, editor. *The Encyclopedia of Drugs and Alcohol.* New York: Macmillan Library Reference, 1995.

Lang, Alan. *Alcohol: Teenage Drinking (The Encyclopedia of Psychoactive Drugs).* New York: Chelsea House, 1992.

Mendelson, Jack, and Nancy Mello. *Alcohol: Use and Abuse in America.* Boston: Little, Brown, 1985.

Monroe, Judy. *Alcohol: The Drug Library.* Springfield, New Jersey: Enslow Publishers, 1994.

Musto, David. "Alcohol in American History." *Scientific American,* April 1996: 78–83.

Postman, N. *Myths, Men, and Beer: An Analysis of Beer Commercials on Broadcast Television—1987.* Washington, DC: AAA Foundation for Traffic Safety, 1987.

Rosenberg, Maxine. *Not My Family: Sharing the Truth about Alcoholism.* New York: Bradbury Press, 1988.

Ryan, Elizabeth. *Straight Talk about Drugs and Alcohol.* New York: Facts on File, 1995.

Ryerson, Eric. *When Your Parent Drinks Too Much: A Book for Teenagers.* New York: Facts on File, 1985.

Siegel, Mark, Alison Landes, and Nancy Jacobs, editors. *Illegal Drugs and Alcohol: America's Anguish* (The Information Series on Current Topics). Wylie, Texas: Information Plus, 1995.

Wekesser, Carol, editor. *Alcoholism* (Current Controversies Books). San Diego: Greenhaven Press, 1994.

INDEX